Dedication

For every coach who listens beyond words.
For every leader who chooses reflection over reaction.
And for every soul learning to be still in a world
that never stops moving.

May this book find you at the exact moment
you need to pause —
and may its ripples remind you of your own.

THE STONE AND THE POND

A JOURNEY OF LISTENING, LEADERSHIP, AND STILLNESS

KISHORE KUMAR THAKUR

Clever Fox® PUBLISHING

Chennai • Bangalore

CLEVER FOX PUBLISHING
Chennai, India

Published by CLEVER FOX PUBLISHING 2025

ISBN: 978-93-7500-738-8

CONTENTS

FOREWORD

I have known Kishore as a friend and a coach who brings presence, curiosity, and quiet depth to every conversation. His initiation into coaching, as he often shares, began during one of his travels — a moment that shaped the path he continues to walk with grace and purpose. He is intense yet thoughtful, simple yet deep, grounded yet passionate about what he does. Kishore embodies the very essence of what he brings forth in this book. His presence itself is transformative — quiet, grounded, and magical.

In *The Stone and the Pond*, Kishore offers another beautiful expression of himself — poetic, authentic, and profoundly human. The narrative begins with a coach preparing to meet a new client and unfolds as a journey of transformation that leads, finally, to legacy. Along the way, it offers countless insights for leaders, coaches, and all who accompany others on their journeys of change.

Through the simple yet evocative metaphor of a stone thrown into a pond, Kishore explores the ripples of change that one moment of awareness can create — and the still, remembering depth of the pond that holds its trace long after.

Listening is the most generous act of leadership.
It is also the most forgotten.

Most people hear to reply. Some hear to fix. Few hear to understand.
Almost no one hears to witness.

This work is both elegant and accessible, written in a reflective and narrative style. It flows through the essential stages of awareness, listening, curiosity, presence, transformation, and legacy — each chapter an unfolding of deeper insight.

What moved me most is how Kishore builds the essence of coaching and leadership from foundation to fulfillment — to the art of letting go. As he reminds us, legacy is not a monument built in our name; it is the quiet continuity of what we once made possible.

Every coach is a stone.
Every conversation, a ripple.
Every listener, a pond remembering itself.

This book is a treasure for everyone who seeks to create change — for leaders of today and tomorrow, for coaches, and for those simply curious about the coaching way. In his characteristic generosity, Kishore shares *The Ripples Framework* — a structure so intuitive that readers can quickly internalize its wisdom, its conversational process, and its quiet power.

I invite you to read this book slowly. Listen to it.
It will begin to speak to you — and, in time, you will hear your own voice in its echoes. That voice will stay with you, like a ripple in your own mind.

As the character Meera says,

"A stone may sink," she thought, "but its impact never does."

Enjoy the experience.

– Kannan Swaminathan,
Executive Coach

PREFACE

The idea for *The Stone and the Pond* came quietly —
not as a plan, but as a feeling.

Over years of coaching and facilitating,
I kept noticing something:
that the greatest shifts in people didn't happen during the moments of brilliance,
but during the moments of silence.

When someone felt truly heard.
When a leader finally paused long enough to listen — not to respond, but to understand.
That's when the real transformation began.

This book is a tribute to those moments —
to every client, colleague, and coach who has taught me that change doesn't always look like action.
Sometimes it looks like awareness.

The metaphor of *the stone and the pond* found me one morning during reflection.
A small stone had fallen into a still pond nearby,
and I watched the ripples move outward — effortless, graceful, endless.
It felt like coaching itself.

We may never see how far our presence travels,
but we can trust that it does.

So this book isn't written *for* you.
It's written *with* you.
Because every reader becomes part of the ripple —
every pause, every reflection, every conversation you have after reading it
is another wave in motion.

Thank you for joining me here —
in the still water.

– Kishore Kumar Thakur

PROLOGUE – THE STONE AND THE POND

The world was still when Meera arrived.
The sun was barely a thought behind the hills, and the mist hung low, curling like soft breath over the valley. The retreat was silent except for the rhythmic hum of insects and the faint rustle of trees.

She walked slowly toward the pond — her favorite spot — the one she always visited before starting a new coaching engagement. The air smelled of wet earth and jasmine. The pond lay before her like glass — perfectly still, perfectly quiet.

She bent down, picked up a small stone, smooth and cool to the touch. For a long moment, she just held it, feeling its weight in her palm. Then, with an easy flick, she dropped it into the water.

The stone sank soundlessly, but the ripples… the ripples spread far and wide. Concentric circles widening, touching everything in their path, until they faded into the edges of the pond.

Meera watched in silence.

"Every conversation," she whispered to herself,
"is like this. You never know how far it travels."

It was something she had learned over years of working with leaders — that real change never happens in boardrooms or strategy documents. It happens quietly, in the pauses between words, in the questions that linger, in the moments when someone feels truly seen.

She remembered her first client, many years ago — a young, defensive manager who thought coaching was a waste of time. Six months later, he was leading with humility and grace. She had lost touch with him since, but once, in a conference hallway, someone mentioned his name and said, *"He changed the culture of our entire region."*

Meera had smiled then. The ripples always find their way.

She sat down on the grass, opened her worn leather notebook, and drew a small circle in the center of a blank page. Around it, she sketched expanding rings. Then, in neat handwriting, she wrote:

"Zenith Global – Arun Mehta."

Her new assignment. A fast-growing conglomerate known for precision, targets, and relentless ambition. She had coached dozens of their senior leaders over the years. But this one — this Arun — came with a note from HR that made her pause:

"High potential, recently promoted, team morale declining, leadership feedback — tense, detached."

She smiled. "The usual symptoms of success," she murmured.

The phone buzzed beside her. A message from Priya, Zenith's HR Director:

'Meera, thank you for taking this on short notice. He's skeptical about coaching, so please tread carefully.'

Meera typed back a single line:

'Every ripple begins with resistance.'

She closed her notebook and looked at the pond again. The water had stilled. Only faint rings remained, melting into the reflection of the rising sun.

She thought of how often leaders mistake control for clarity, activity for impact. Coaching, she knew, was the opposite — a practice of surrendering control to allow reflection.

She spoke softly, as if to the pond itself:

"The surface must be still before the depth can be seen."

Her driver called from a distance — the car was ready. She stood, dusted off her shawl, and looked once more at the water. It mirrored her face — calm, unhurried, ageless in its quiet certainty.

Somewhere inside, she felt the familiar mixture of anticipation and humility. Every new engagement was a mystery — she could never predict what would unfold. But she trusted the process. She trusted the ripples.

As she walked back along the path lined with banyan trees, a pair of herons glided across the pond, their wings carving delicate lines in the water.

The ripples returned — larger this time, merging, crossing, overlapping — like conversations echoing across lives.

Meera smiled.

"A stone may sink," she thought,
"But its impact never does."

She got into the car, her notebook resting on her lap. The road to the city curved ahead like a question waiting to be asked.

By the time the pond returned to stillness, the first ripple of change had already begun — though no one, not even Meera, could yet see how far it would travel.

Coach's Reflection Ripples and Readiness

I have learned that not everyone is ready to be coached.
And that's perfectly fine.

People often meet us where *their* story is — not where we wish it would be.
Some arrive curious, open, ready to explore.
Most arrive cautious, armoured in success, speaking a language of results and deadlines.

But beneath every performance report lies a quiet ache — a longing to feel *enough*.
That's where the work begins.

Coaching isn't about teaching leaders what to do;
it's about reminding them who they already are.

Sometimes that reminder comes through silence.
Sometimes, through a single question that unsettles what they thought they knew.

And then, slowly, the surface breaks.
The water that was once still begins to ripple.
The mind that was restless begins to rest.
And from that stillness — awareness arises.

Awareness is the first ripple.
It doesn't shout.
It simply *moves*.

And once it begins, nothing — and no one — remains quite the same.

PART I

THE SURFACE

The First Ripple of Awareness

"Every ripple starts as a disturbance."

CHAPTER 1

THE STONE

A SMALL DISTURBANCE

"Every ripple begins with something that disturbs the surface."

The promotion should have felt like a triumph.
A new title, a larger team, another floor closer to the boardroom.

But as Arun stared at the congratulatory emails filling his inbox, he felt nothing.
The applause was loud.
The silence inside him was louder.

Somewhere, unseen, the first stone had entered the water.

The rain had stopped, but the city hadn't noticed.
Cars hissed along wet asphalt, honking through puddles.
Inside Zenith Global's gleaming headquarters, everything looked polished — the glass walls, the marble floors, even the smiles.

On the fourteenth floor, in a corner office with a view of the skyline, sat **Arun Mehta**, newly promoted Vice President of

Operations.
The plaque on his desk still looked new, the kind that catches the light too easily.
Beside it lay a half-drunk cup of coffee, cold now.

His inbox overflowed, his phone blinked with messages, but his attention drifted elsewhere — out the window, to the rain clouds dispersing above the towers.
He should have felt proud.
Everyone told him he should.

The promotion was the culmination of years of late nights, weekend calls, and performance reviews that read like victory speeches.
But that morning, when the CEO had congratulated him, the applause from his team had felt distant — polite, hollow, rehearsed.
He'd smiled, of course. He always did.
But once the crowd dispersed, the quiet emptiness behind the success returned — heavier than before.

He turned back to his screen. Another email from HR.
The subject line read: **"Executive Coaching Engagement – Mandatory Orientation."**

Arun sighed. "Not this again," he muttered.

It wasn't his first exposure to coaching.
Years ago, as part of a leadership program, a cheerful facilitator had asked everyone to *"reflect on their values."*

He'd found it indulgent — a waste of time for people with real work to do.

But this time it wasn't optional. His boss, Sanjay Rao, had made that clear.

Earlier That Morning

"Arun," Sanjay had said, adjusting his cufflinks, "you've earned this role.
But we need you to… how do I put it… connect better with people."

He paused. "Your results are brilliant, but your team morale — not so much."

Arun tried not to roll his eyes. "We're in operations, Sanjay. We're not running a therapy group."

Sanjay smiled knowingly. "I said the same thing once.
Then I learned the hard way that even operations run on emotion."

He leaned closer. "Don't fight this. HR's bringing in Meera Anand. She's one of the best. Think of it as… sharpening the saw."

Arun forced a nod. "Sure."

But as he left the room, irritation simmered.
Coaching felt like a punishment disguised as development.
He'd built his career on logic, performance, and control.
Now, someone wanted to talk about *feelings?*

The Meeting That Followed

At 10 a.m., he walked into a team huddle.
The room fell silent the moment he entered.
He noticed it — the stiffness in shoulders, the guarded expressions.

He began briskly. "Let's review last week's numbers."
They did — mechanically.

Riya, the intern, hesitated before offering a suggestion.
Arun cut her off mid-sentence, unintentionally.
The air thinned again.

When the meeting ended, he overheard someone whisper, "I miss the old Arun."

Old Arun?
He wasn't sure what they meant.

Back in his office, he stared again at the email from HR.
"Executive Coaching."

He clicked it open.

The Message

Dear Arun,
We're pleased to introduce you to your leadership coach, Ms. Meera Anand.
Your first session is scheduled for next Wednesday at 11:00 a.m.
Meera has extensive experience in transformational leadership development and executive behavior change.

Best,
Priya Nair
Director, People & Culture, Zenith Global

He stared at the phrase *"behavior change."*
He didn't like it.

He was being *fixed.* That's how it felt.

Still, he exhaled, clicked **Add to Calendar**, and shut his laptop.

For a moment, he leaned back and closed his eyes.
The faint hum of the air conditioner filled the room — a steady, artificial breeze against a restless mind.

In the quiet, a memory surfaced.
He was ten, skipping stones at a pond near his grandfather's house.
Each stone made ripples that expanded until they vanished.

His grandfather had said, "Notice how far they go, even from one small flick of your hand?"

Back then, he hadn't cared.
He'd just wanted to see how many skips he could get before the stone sank.

Now, decades later, surrounded by deadlines and performance charts, he wondered:
When did he stop noticing the ripples?
And who would help him see them again?

The intercom beeped.
"Sir," said his assistant, "the CEO wants to see you briefly."

Arun straightened his tie, grabbed his notepad, and walked toward the elevator.
The corridor lights reflected on the glass walls — so bright they almost hurt his eyes.

From the lobby, the city looked alive again.
The rain had washed everything clean.
Except him.

Some promotions lift you up.
Others reveal how heavy you've become.

He didn't know it yet,
But that heaviness was about to be lifted —
not by applause, not by strategy,
But by a question he wasn't ready to answer.

Coach's Reflection – On Resistance

Every leader arrives armoured.
The armour is rarely visible, but it's there — woven from experience, fear, and pride.

It glints through polished confidence, sharp replies, and the impatience to move faster.
To many, coaching feels like standing still — and stillness, for the driven, feels like failure.

But resistance is not rejection.
It is the soul's way of testing sincerity.

When a leader resists, they're not saying "I won't change."
They're really saying, "Can I trust you with what I hide?"

The first work of a coach, then, is not to push — but to wait.
To wait without an agenda, to listen without wanting.

Because when listening replaces persuasion, defenses melt on their own.

And when the armour finally softens, even slightly —
That's when the first ripple begins.

CHAPTER 2

THE RELUCTANT COACHEE

THE FIRST CONVERSATION

"The first ripple is rarely gentle.
It disturbs before it transforms."

The room smelled faintly of lemongrass and paper.
Soft light filtered through the tall windows of Zenith Global's executive lounge —
A deliberate attempt, perhaps, to make conversations like this one feel less corporate, less cold.

Arun glanced at his watch. 10:58 a.m.
He hated being early, but he hated being late even more.

He scanned the room — a low table, two armchairs, a bowl of white stones, and a carafe of water.
The kind of minimalist setup that made him feel exposed.
There was no desk to hide behind, no laptop, no spreadsheet to summon control.

He was still studying the framed quote on the wall —
"Change begins the moment you decide to pause." —
When a quiet voice interrupted his thoughts.

"Good morning, Mr. Mehta."

He turned.

She stood at the doorway — a woman in her early fifties, dressed in pale grey, hair tied neatly, presence calm but alert. No clipboard. No laptop. Just a small notebook and a serene half-smile.

"I'm Meera," she said, setting her notebook down. "Thank you for meeting with me."

"Of course," Arun replied automatically. "HR said this is… part of the leadership program."

"Yes," she said, taking her seat. "Though I prefer to think of it as a conversation — not a program."

He managed a polite smile. "I'm not sure how these usually work. I assume you'll need to understand my role and challenges—"

She lifted a hand gently, as if pausing the rhythm of his sentence.
"We can talk about all of that," she said. "But may I ask something first?"

"Sure," he said, leaning back.

Meera looked at him steadily, not unkindly.
"When did you last feel proud of your work?"

The question hung in the air like a held breath.

Arun blinked. "Proud?"

He tried to recall — a project closed, a bonus achieved, an award maybe — but each memory felt distant, transactional.

"Honestly," he said after a moment, "I don't think about pride. I focus on outcomes."

Meera nodded slowly. "So outcomes, not emotions."

He shrugged. "That's what gets results."

She smiled softly. "Perhaps. But results are usually emotions wearing numbers."

He frowned slightly, unsure if she was joking.
She wasn't.

"May I ask," she continued, "what result brought you here — to this conversation?"

He almost laughed. "I was told to."

"And how do you feel about that?"

He hesitated. The words came sharper than intended.
"Honestly? I think it's unnecessary. My team respects me, even if they don't always like me. I deliver. That's what matters."

Meera didn't flinch. She simply listened — really listened — in a way he wasn't used to.
No judgment. No counterargument. Just still attention.

After a moment, she said quietly,
"Sometimes people respect us because they have to.
And sometimes, they trust us because they want to.
The two are not the same."

The silence that followed wasn't awkward — it was alive.

For the first time in years, Arun felt the discomfort of being truly seen.
He reached for his coffee cup, just to do something with his hands. It was cold.

Meera glanced at her notebook but didn't write anything.

"I'm not here to fix you," she said gently. "Coaching isn't repair work. It's reflection work."

Arun looked up. "Reflection work?"

"Yes. Like holding up a mirror — not to judge, but to notice."

He exhaled, uncertain whether to feel relieved or cornered.
He wanted to say something clever, something to reestablish control, but instead he found himself asking,
"And what happens after noticing?"

Meera smiled. "Ah. That's when choice begins."

For a long moment, neither spoke.
Outside, rainclouds gathered again, darkening the glass walls.

The hum of the air conditioner filled the space between their silences.

Finally, she said, "Our next session will be next week. Until then, I'd like you to try one small thing."

Arun raised an eyebrow. "Homework?"

She laughed lightly. "If you like, yes. But it's very simple. The next time you're in a meeting, try listening without planning your response."

He almost smiled. "That's it?"

"That's it."

He nodded, eager to leave, but something in her tone — calm, unhurried — made him pause.
She added softly,
"Listening isn't silence. It's presence. There's a difference."

He gave a polite nod and stood up. "Thank you, Ms. Anand. I'll… try."

As he turned to leave, she said,
"And Arun — pride isn't the opposite of humility.
It's the echo of purpose. You'll find it when you stop chasing."

He stopped briefly at the door but didn't look back.

When he reached his car, he realized he'd forgotten his umbrella. He didn't go back for it.

He started the engine but didn't drive.
Outside, the rain blurred the lights into slow-moving circles.

Her words echoed like ripples from a distant stone:
"Listening isn't silence. It's presence."

He didn't know why, but they unsettled him — not because they were wrong,
but because they felt right.

Some conversations don't end when you leave the room.
They travel with you — quietly, persistently —
until you're ready to hear them again.

Coach's Reflection – On Listening

Listening is the most generous act of leadership.
It is also the most forgotten.

Most people hear to reply.
Some hear to fix.
Few hear to understand.
Almost no one hears to witness.

True listening asks for surrender — not of intellect, but of ego.
It requires you to stop performing the role of the expert and return to being a learner of the moment.

In coaching, listening is not the space between questions.
It is the coaching.

Words are only pebbles;
listening is the water that allows them to ripple.

When a leader truly listens — without interrupting, without rescuing, without rehearsing — something sacred happens.
The other person begins to listen to themselves.

And that, more than any technique or tool, is where transformation begins.

"What begins as resistance often becomes reflection."

PART II

THE RIPPLES

Where Awareness Meets Relationship

"Change flows outward, one conversation at a time."

CHAPTER 3

THE MIRROR OF SILENCE

WHEN AWARENESS BEGINS TO LISTEN

"The mirror never speaks — it only waits for you to look long enough to see."

It had been three days since the conversation, and Meera's words still echoed in his head.
"Listening isn't silence. It's presence."

Arun tried to ignore them.
He buried himself in work, in numbers, in meetings, in the endless rhythm of tasks that usually numbed thought.
But somehow, every pause — every quiet moment between calls — carried a faint echo of that sentence.

The Meeting

It was Thursday morning — the weekly operations review.
He walked into the conference room, laptop in hand, ready with the latest metrics.
His team was already there — Dev, Riya, and a few others.

The usual energy was missing — or maybe he was just noticing it for the first time.
The polite nods, the quick shuffling of papers, the faint tension in the air — it all seemed louder today.

"Let's begin," he said, clicking through the slides.

Dev presented updates, efficient as always.
Riya hesitated when her turn came. She started explaining her analysis of a customer issue, but halfway through, she faltered.

"I think the problem might be—"

"Let's not guess," Arun said quickly. "We'll need data before making assumptions."

Her voice trailed off. "Yes, of course."

A silence fell. The air conditioner hummed faintly.
And then it happened — a flicker of recognition.

He heard his own tone.
He saw Riya's shoulders drop, her confidence retreating like a tide.
He felt the very ripple he had just created — one of retreat, not growth.

For a moment, the room seemed to hold its breath with him.
For the first time, he didn't brush it off. He noticed.

After the Meeting

When the room emptied, Arun stayed behind, staring at the now-blank screen.

Something in his chest felt tight — not guilt exactly, but awareness.

He remembered Meera's calm face, the stillness in her eyes when she'd said:
"Listening is presence."

He realized he hadn't been present at all.
He'd been managing, directing, protecting results — not people.

He picked up his pen and, without thinking, opened his notebook.
On a blank page, he wrote a single word:

Listening.

Then below it:
What am I afraid will happen if I stop talking?

He stared at the question.
It wasn't one Meera had asked.
It had come from somewhere inside him.
He stared at the words until they stopped being a question and became a mirror.

The Evening

That evening, he skipped his usual after-hours emails and drove home early.
His daughter, Anya, was sitting on the floor, surrounded by sketchbooks.

"Papa, look!" she said, showing him a page of colored circles that overlapped like ripples in water.

He smiled. "That's beautiful. What's it called?"

She thought for a moment. "It's called *What Happens When You Wait.*"

He froze for a second.
She was eight.
How did she know to call it that?

He ruffled her hair gently, but her words stayed with him — the strange coincidence, the timing, the quiet truth of it.

The Night Journal

Later that night, long after everyone had gone to sleep, he sat at his desk.
The city lights spilled through the curtains, scattering across the floor.

He opened his notebook again and began to write — not reports, not goals — just thoughts.

"I noticed how I interrupt.
How I finish people's sentences.
I don't mean to. I just… want to move faster.
But maybe at that speed, I'm losing something — or someone."

He paused, staring at what he had written.
It felt uncomfortable to admit, but also strangely freeing.

He remembered Meera's words again:
"Reflection isn't judgment; it's noticing."

He exhaled. Closed the notebook.
For the first time in years, he felt a kind of quiet he couldn't name — not peace exactly, but presence.

It was small, fragile, but real.
He didn't know it yet, but that moment — that pause — was his first ripple.
Somewhere deep inside, something had started to listen back.

Before behavior changes, awareness must awaken.
And before awareness awakens, silence must be allowed to speak.

Coach's Reflection – On Awareness

"Awareness is the first conversation we have with truth."

Awareness is the softest kind of truth.
It doesn't demand. It reveals.

Most people seek transformation through action —
new goals, new plans, new habits.
But change begins not in movement,
it begins with noticing.

Awareness is the mirror we spend our whole lives avoiding.
We fear what it might show us — our impatience, our patterns, our unmet needs.
But the mirror is never cruel.
It simply reflects what is.

In coaching, awareness is not the answer — it's the doorway.
It is the breath between reaction and response,
the pause before the next ripple forms.

And once you see yourself clearly,
you can no longer pretend not to.

That is both the gift and the burden of awakening.

Awareness does not change you instantly.
It simply refuses to let you stay the same.

CHAPTER 4

THE FIRST RIPPLE

THE WEIGHT OF WORDS

"Every word is a pebble.
Some sink. Some ripple forever."

Monday arrived with its usual rush — unread emails, back-to-back calls, and a to-do list that already looked impossible.
But something in Arun had shifted.
He couldn't explain it, but there was a quiet observer inside him now — watching, noticing, pausing.

He'd reread his notebook the night before. The line stared back at him:

"What am I afraid will happen if I stop talking?"

The question had no easy answer.
So he carried it with him into the new week.

The Team Huddle

The morning meeting began as usual.
The team sat around the oval table, laptops open, caffeine in hand.

Dev was summarizing numbers; Riya was scrolling nervously through her slides.

Normally, Arun would take control — correct, direct, conclude. But today, he decided to try something different.

He remembered Meera's words: *"Listening isn't silence. It's presence."*
So he listened. He decided to listen not to the words, but to the spaces between them.

He noticed Dev's clipped tone when he mentioned "unrealistic targets."
He noticed how Riya avoided eye contact when speaking about a failed experiment.
He noticed the fatigue in the room — not physical, but emotional.

For the first time, he saw what was always there.

"Riya," he said gently when she finished, "tell me more about what didn't work. What do you think we missed?"

Riya blinked, surprised.
Usually, this was where he'd move to the next slide or point out what went wrong.

"I… think we didn't ask the customer enough questions," she said slowly. "We assumed what they wanted instead of listening."

Dev smirked. "We didn't have time for that."

Arun turned to him. "What if we made time?"

Dev frowned. "Sir, with respect, we're drowning in targets."

"I know," Arun said. "But maybe that's the problem — we're so busy doing that we've stopped asking."

The room went quiet.
Something in his tone — calm, not defensive — caught their attention.

Riya looked at him, uncertain but encouraged.
"Could we try one round of customer calls this week?" she asked. "Just listening — not pitching."

Arun nodded. "Let's do that."

It wasn't a big decision.
There were no metrics attached, no announcement, no celebration.
But in that moment, something unspoken shifted in the room.
It was as if the air had cleared.

For the first time, the meeting had ended not with decisions, but with connection.

Later That Evening

Back in his office, Arun sat alone for a few minutes after everyone had left.
The building's hum was softer now — quieter somehow.

He thought about what had just happened.
No one had said anything extraordinary.
But the conversation had *felt* different — lighter, truer.

He opened his notebook again and wrote:

"I didn't interrupt today. I asked. And they answered."

He smiled faintly.

He didn't know it yet, but that small act of listening had already begun to spread.
Riya would leave the meeting energized, telling her colleague, "He actually listened today."
Dev, skeptical but thoughtful, would replay the exchange in his head, wondering if he'd been too harsh.
And somewhere deep within Arun, a quiet pride flickered — not the pride of performance, but of presence.

The Coach's Note

That evening, Meera sat in her own study, sipping tea as she wrote in her journal.
She didn't know exactly what had transpired in Arun's meeting, but she sensed it.
After years of coaching, she could always feel the first ripple — a subtle vibration in the silence between sessions.

She wrote:

"The first ripple is not visible.
It begins the moment someone listens to themselves listening. That is when silence starts to teach."

She closed her notebook, smiling softly.

Change doesn't announce itself.
It arrives disguised as a moment that could have been ignored.

Coach's Reflection – On Small Shifts

Change rarely begins with grand decisions.
It begins with the tiniest interruption of habit —
a pause before reacting,
a question instead of an answer,
a breath before the next word.

The human mind craves momentum.
We confuse movement with progress,
and noise with impact.
But transformation has a different rhythm —
slow, steady, almost invisible at first.

Small shifts look insignificant in the moment.
But over time, they alter the course of everything around them.

A leader who listens once, listens again.
A team that feels heard begins to speak.
A culture that starts to speak begins to heal.

The ripple begins not with power,
but with permission —
the permission to slow down, to see, to sense.

In the language of leadership, these shifts are whispers.
In the language of life, they are revolutions.

The smallest change in presence can create the largest change in possibility.

CHAPTER 5

LISTENING BEYOND SOUND

WHEN PRESENCE BECOMES CONNECTION

"True listening hears what isn't said."

It started almost unnoticed.

The Monday meeting felt… different.
Not because the agenda had changed — it hadn't — but because *Arun* had.

He still carried his notes, still wore his crisp shirt, still followed the numbers.
But when the meeting began, he did something unusual for him —

he didn't start talking.

He looked around the table, meeting each person's eyes a moment longer than usual.
"Let's begin," he said softly, "with what you've been noticing — not just in the data, but in the work itself."

There was a pause.
People glanced at each other, unsure what he meant.

Dev was the first to speak. "We've hit targets in three regions," he said. "Though customer engagement's dipping slightly."

Riya added softly, "Some of our clients said we're efficient, but not easy to talk to."

Normally, Arun would have jumped in with a solution, or at least a counterpoint.
Instead, he leaned back slightly, nodded, and said,

"Say more about that, Riya."

The room shifted — almost imperceptibly.
She blinked, caught off guard, but continued,
"I think we've become so focused on delivery that we don't build connection. They trust our work, but not us."

Arun nodded again. "And how do you feel about that?"

The word *feel* hung in the air like a foreign language. It was the first time the meeting felt human.
But no one laughed.

"I feel," she said slowly, "that we could listen more. Understand what matters to them."

The room was silent — not awkwardly, but curiously.
Even Dev looked thoughtful.

The First Conversation That Wasn't About Performance

Over the next few weeks, the meetings changed subtly.
There were still charts, metrics, deadlines — but there was also space.
Space for questions, for uncertainty, for honesty.

Riya began taking the lead in discussions she'd once avoided.
Dev, though skeptical, started pausing before replying — an almost miraculous development.
The junior analysts, usually quiet, began volunteering small ideas.

No one called it "culture change."
It just happened — like sunlight gradually softening a dark room.

Arun began to notice things he had once missed:
the small spark in Riya's eyes when her idea landed,
the relief on Dev's face when he wasn't blamed for a delay,
the faint laughter that started to return in the breaks between meetings.

He didn't announce this shift to anyone.
He just kept listening.

And the more he listened,
the more others began to listen too.

An Unexpected Moment

One afternoon, during a review with his regional managers, Dev said something that made Arun pause.

"I tried your thing," Dev said matter-of-factly.

"My thing?" Arun asked.

"You know, listening. I didn't jump to fix. Just let the client talk. And guess what? He ended up giving us what we wanted without me asking."

The room laughed lightly. Arun smiled.
"That's not *my* thing, Dev," he said. "It's just something we forgot."

Later, as the meeting ended, Dev lingered.
"Sir," he said quietly, "I have to admit — you've changed. I didn't think people like us could slow down."

Arun smiled, genuinely. "Neither did I."

Dev hesitated. "Feels better though."

And in that small, awkward admission, the ripple grew stronger.

At Home

That night, as Arun was helping Anya with her homework, she asked,
"Papa, why do you listen so much these days?"

He looked up, surprised. "Do I?"

She nodded solemnly. "Before, you answered fast. Now you wait."

He laughed softly. "Maybe I'm learning."

She returned to her book. "Then you must be a good student."

He smiled — and realized she was right.

Meanwhile, at the Pond

Across the city, Meera sat by her balcony plants, writing her evening notes.
She didn't know the details, but she sensed the shift.
Years of coaching had taught her that when awareness takes root, silence follows differently.

She wrote:

"A room changes not when the leader speaks,
but when they stop needing to."

She closed her notebook and whispered a quiet thank-you — not to the universe, but to the process. Some ripples travel farther than the eye can follow.

When a leader learns to listen, a team learns to breathe.
And when a team breathes together, it begins to dream again.

Coach's Reflection – "On Trust"

Trust is never built in words.
It is built in the spaces between them.

We often believe trust is earned through promises kept or performances delivered.
But real trust begins long before that —
in the first moment, someone feels safe enough to speak the truth.

People don't open up because they are told to.
They open up because they feel heard, not judged —
because they sense your stillness is large enough to hold their fear.

A leader's silence can be terrifying if it hides judgment,
but healing if it holds presence.

Trust grows slowly —
like a seed that only sprouts when the soil feels safe.

And when trust finally takes root,
communication no longer needs translation.
Teams breathe easier.
People return to themselves.

The secret is simple,
but not easy:
To listen, not for what is said,
but for what is trying to be said.

Trust is not built by convincing others to believe in you.
It's built when you start believing in them — before they do.

PART III

THE DEEP WATER

Where Awareness Becomes Practice

"Stillness is not the absence of motion, but its mastery."

CHAPTER 6

RIPPLES IN THE WORKPLACE

THE PILOT THAT CHANGED EVERYTHING

When one person chooses to listen, an entire system exhales."

The idea was simple.
Almost too simple.

One Wednesday morning, Riya walked into Arun's office, notebook in hand. She was nervous — not because her idea was radical, but because it wasn't backed by data, projections, or a PowerPoint. Just intuition.

"Sir," she began hesitantly, "do you remember how we discussed listening to our customers more deeply?"

Arun looked up from his laptop, smiling. "Yes, I do."

She took a breath. "I've been thinking… what if we run a pilot project — just three clients — where we don't pitch anything for a week? We just listen. Ask questions. Understand their challenges. That's it."

Arun raised an eyebrow. "No selling? No proposing solutions?"

Riya shook her head. "Just listening."

He leaned back, intrigued.
A few months ago, he would have dismissed it instantly.
Now, he felt a quiet curiosity.

"What's the goal?" he asked.

She smiled nervously. "To see what happens when we stop talking… and start hearing"

He chuckled softly. "You've been spending too much time in our meetings, Riya."

"Maybe," she said, blushing, "but I really believe it could work."

He nodded. "Do it."

She blinked. "Really?"

"Yes. Three clients. Three conversations. Just listening. Let's call it… the *Ripple Pilot.*"

Her eyes lit up. "Ripple?"

He smiled. "It's just a word that's been following me lately."

The Week of Silence

Over the next seven days, Riya and two colleagues met with three long-term clients.
They didn't pitch a new product. They didn't defend the old one.
They just asked questions — open, curious, human questions.

"What's been hard for you this quarter?"
"What do you wish your vendors understood about your world?"
"If you could change one thing about how we work together, what would it be?"

And then — they listened.

At first, the clients were puzzled.
No slides? No targets? No agenda?
But slowly, the conversations began to flow.

One client said, "You're the first vendor who's ever asked what *we* need, not just what *you* can deliver."

Another shared an internal challenge that explained months of miscommunication — something that had never surfaced before.
The third, touched by the sincerity, invited Zenith Global to co-create a new process — something unheard of in their relationship.

Riya took careful notes, her nervousness replaced by awe.
It was working.

The Review Meeting

At the end of the week, Riya stood in the conference room, presenting her findings.
This time, there was no trembling in her voice.

"Our clients opened up in ways we hadn't expected. They shared pain points we didn't know existed. And they thanked us — for listening."

She looked around the room, her voice steady. "It turns out people don't resist change. They resist *not being heard.*"

There was a brief silence.
Then, to her astonishment, Dev — ever the skeptic — leaned forward.

"This could be a game-changer," he said quietly. "If we understand them better, we can anticipate their needs. It's not soft — it's smart."

Arun nodded, a small smile on his lips. "Exactly."

For a moment, he didn't speak further. He simply looked at his team — Riya, Dev, the analysts — and felt something he hadn't felt in years.

Pride.
Not in the numbers, not in the outcomes, but in the *energy.*

He realized the room no longer felt heavy.
It felt lighter, as if the walls themselves had begun to listen. It felt alive.

After the Meeting

When everyone left, Arun stayed behind again.
He looked at the empty chairs, the faint hum of the projector, the sunlight spilling through the blinds.

He remembered Meera's first question:

"When did you last feel proud of your work?"

He smiled quietly. *Now,* he thought. *Right now.*

He realized that pride had returned, not as ego, but as empathy. It was no longer about being right — it was about being real.

He opened his notebook and wrote:

"Riya's pilot worked. Three clients, three conversations, no agenda — just attention.
The results were better than any strategy deck."

And below that, almost like a confession:

"I didn't create this. I just created the space for it."

Meanwhile, Across Town

Meera sat in her quiet study, a cup of tea warming her palms. Something in her intuition told her to pause mid-sip. She smiled faintly.
She didn't know what was happening in that office, but she sensed movement — a new ripple forming.

She opened her journal and wrote:

"When silence replaces certainty, creativity reappears — like light returning after a long storm.

A leader's greatest contribution is often the space they no longer fill."

That night, as Arun drove home, the rain returned.
The city lights shimmered across the wet roads like ripples in motion.
At a red light, he caught his own reflection in the car window.

He looked tired, yes — but softer somehow. Lighter.
It struck him that for years, he had been speaking to be understood.
Now, for the first time, he was listening to understand.

He smiled to himself, watching the raindrops trace quiet circles on the windshield.

Somewhere, unseen, the pond rippled again.

Leadership doesn't begin when people follow you.
It begins when they start trusting themselves in your presence.

Coach's Reflection – On Empowerment

Empowerment is not something we give.
It's something we stop taking away.

So many leaders say,
"I empower my team."
But true empowerment is not a declaration.
It's an absence of control, of fear, of ego.

When we stop speaking for others,
they find their own voice.
When we stop fixing,
they start creating.
When we stop rescuing,
they learn to rise.

Empowerment is not a handout.
It's a hand withdrawn —
a space left open for growth to fill.

Coaching lives in that space.
The silence after the question.
The pause before the answer.
The trust that what wants to emerge, will.

The real measure of leadership is not how many people follow you —
but how many no longer need to.

The moment you stop needing to be the center of the ripple,
you realize you've already created one.

CHAPTER 7

THE POWER OF REFLECTION

WHEN RIPPLES MEET RESISTANCE

"Still water isn't weak. It's just learned not to fight every wave."

The following quarter began with a familiar rhythm — reviews, reports, results.
But something beneath the surface had changed.
Arun's team felt more alive, more collaborative, more trusting.
Even the data reflected it — fewer errors, faster problem-solving, more innovation.

But not everyone saw it that way.

At the senior leadership review, **Sanjay Rao**, Arun's boss, flipped through the latest slides with a frown.
"Yes, Arun," he said slowly, "I see the metrics are steady. But this new 'listening' approach — it's slowing down decision-making."

Arun met his gaze calmly. "I don't believe it's slowing us down, sir. It's making our decisions more sustainable."

Sanjay sighed. "That's not what I meant. I mean… this coaching stuff — it's too soft. We're not a wellness center. We're an operations company. We deliver."

There it was — the echo of the old culture.
Efficiency over empathy.
Speed over substance.

Arun took a slow breath. "I understand your concern," he said. "But our last three client renewals came directly from the pilot approach. Listening created trust. Trust created results."

Sanjay closed the file. "Be careful, Arun. Don't lose your edge trying to be liked."

He didn't argue. He simply felt the weight of the sentence settle like an old coat he no longer wished to wear.

He meant it as advice. But to Arun, it felt like a quiet warning.

The Conversation That Lingered

Later that evening, Arun sat in his car, watching the office lights fade through the rain.
Sanjay's words echoed: *"Don't lose your edge."*

For years, his edge had been his armor — quick thinking, control, results.
But now, that armor felt heavier than protective.
He thought of Meera, of her calm eyes, of her words:

"Coaching isn't about being soft. It's about being still in the storm."

He decided to call her.

The Call

"Good evening, Meera," he said. "Do you have a minute?"

"Of course," she replied. Her voice always sounded like still water.

"I had a difficult review," he began. "My boss thinks I'm slowing things down. That this whole approach — listening, empowering — isn't practical. I don't know if I should hold my ground or go back to the old way."

There was silence on the line — the kind that wasn't empty, but full.

Then she said,

"When the old current meets the new ripple, turbulence is natural. Don't mistake resistance for failure."

He exhaled. "It just feels like I'm being tested."

"You are," she said gently. "But not by your boss — by your own conviction."

He was quiet. "Conviction?"

"Yes," she said. "You asked your team to trust themselves. Now the question is — do you trust yourself enough to continue?"

He leaned back in his seat, staring at the dashboard lights.
"I want to," he said quietly. "But part of me still wants approval."

Meera's tone softened further. "Approval is a habit, too. Leaders often trade authenticity for applause — without realizing it."

He nodded, more to himself than to her.

"What do I do?" he asked finally.

She paused. "Stay curious, not defensive. And remember — turbulence is just the pond remembering it was once a river."

The call ended, but her words lingered long after the line went silent.

The Meeting That Followed

A week later, Sanjay visited Arun's floor for an unscheduled check-in.
He noticed the mood — laughter, open discussions, a relaxed energy.
It unsettled him slightly.

"Looks like a café, not an ops floor," he muttered under his breath.

Riya overheard and smiled politely. "Would you like a coffee, sir?"

Sanjay looked at her — surprised by her confidence — and then at Arun.
"You've created quite a culture here," he said, half-admiring, half-dubious.

Arun replied evenly, "I've just made it safe for people to care again."

Sanjay didn't respond. He looked around once more, then walked away — perhaps with more questions than answers.

Arun watched him go, his pulse steady.
He didn't need approval anymore.
He needed alignment — with himself.

That night, he wrote in his notebook:

"The old current tested me today. I didn't fight it. I just let the ripple hold."

And below that:

"Stillness isn't passivity. It's conviction without noise."

He closed the notebook and smiled faintly.
He realized Meera was right — resistance wasn't the enemy.
It was evidence that change was real.

Meanwhile

In her quiet home office, Meera reread Arun's last message.
She smiled, sensing his steadiness.

She wrote in her journal:

"True growth is when the leader no longer looks for the coach —

because the coach now lives in their own stillness."

She placed her pen down and whispered,

"The ripple holds."

Resistance is not the end of progress.
It is the proof that progress has begun.

Coach's Reflection – On Conviction

Conviction is not loud.
It doesn't shout, argue, or prove.
It breathes. Quietly.

When the old ways push back — as they always do —
the temptation is to defend the new.
To explain, justify, convince.
But real conviction doesn't seek agreement.
It stands gently, like a tree rooted in knowing.

Conviction is the stillness beneath the storm.
It doesn't resist the wind — it allows it to pass.

Leaders often confuse conviction with certainty.
Certainty closes. Conviction opens.
Certainty says, "I'm right."
Conviction says, "I'm clear."

In coaching, we call this the center.
That quiet, unshakeable space inside every human being
that knows — even when the noise outside grows louder.

When a leader finds that center,
they stop reacting.
They start responding.

And that difference — between reaction and response —
is the distance between control and trust,

between force and influence,
between compliance and commitment.

Conviction doesn't come from knowing you'll succeed.
It comes from knowing you're aligned, even if you don't.

CHAPTER 8

THE SECOND RIPPLE

WHEN STILLNESS SPREADS

"Presence is contagious. When one person slows down, others remember how."

The morning sunlight poured through the office windows, glinting off polished glass and coffee mugs.
It looked like any other day at Zenith Global — except something, again, had shifted.
This time, not in Arun.
In **Dev.**

"He arrived early — a rare event — and lingered by the edge of Riya's desk.

"Can I run something by you?" he asked.

Riya blinked. Dev never asked for input. He usually *gave* it.
"Of course," she said.

"I have a client review today," he said, adjusting his cufflinks.
"They're upset about the timeline. Normally, I'd explain our process, defend the plan. But…" he hesitated, "I thought maybe

I'd just ask what's bothering them first. You know — your pilot thing."

Riya smiled. "You mean the listening thing?"

He smirked. "Yeah, that."

The Meeting

The client was indeed frustrated.
Their tone sharp, their body language closed.

Dev sat across the table, hands folded, fighting the urge to argue.
Instead, he took a slow breath — something he'd seen Arun do — and asked calmly,

"Can you tell me more about what's making this difficult for you?"

The client stopped mid-sentence, surprised.
"Well… mostly, we feel like we're always firefighting. We don't get to plan together — it's always us reacting to your timelines."

Dev nodded slowly. "I see. That sounds exhausting."

The man across from him exhaled, his tone softening. "It is."

"What would a better partnership look like?" Dev asked.

For the next twenty minutes, the client talked — freely, openly.
By the end of the conversation, the tension had dissolved – replaced by a new workflow they had co-created together.

When Dev returned to the office, his face carried an expression no one had seen before — stillness, not smugness.

Arun was standing by the coffee machine when Dev walked in. "How did it go?" Arun asked.

Dev took a sip of his tea. "Different," he said. "No defending, no arguing. Just listening. And you know what?"
He paused.
"They thanked me."

Arun smiled quietly. "Feels strange, doesn't it? Doing less, yet achieving more."

Dev chuckled. "I wouldn't go that far. But maybe you're onto something."

They shared a small laugh — not the polite kind, but one of genuine connection.

The Lunch Table

That afternoon, something unusual happened.
For the first time in months, the entire team had lunch together — not a quick bite between emails, but a real meal.

Someone cracked a joke about their new "Zen mode."
Riya rolled her eyes but smiled.
Even Dev laughed.

As Arun watched them — eating, talking, relaxed — he realized the culture wasn't *changing* anymore.
It *had changed.*

He hadn't announced a program, written a memo, or held a workshop.
He'd simply started listening.
And now, listening was multiplying.

Later That Evening

The day had ended without drama, but something irreversible had begun.

At home, he told Meera about the day's events during their check-in call.

"So," she said, smiling through the phone, "Dev listened."

"He did," Arun said, almost proudly. "He didn't argue. He didn't fix. He just… listened. And it worked."

"And how do you feel?" she asked.

Arun paused. "Honestly?"
He smiled faintly. "Like I'm not carrying it all anymore."

Meera nodded, though he couldn't see her.

"When leadership stops being about control," she said softly, "It starts being about contagion."

"Contagion?"

"Yes," she said. "Presence spreads. Just like pressure does. And the difference between the two defines a culture."

He was quiet for a long moment. "You're right."

"Arun," she said gently, "this is the second ripple. The moment when your way becomes their way. Protect it, but don't possess it."

He smiled. "I think I understand."

That night, he opened his notebook and wrote:

"Dev listened today. Riya smiled today. The room breathed today.
I think this is what culture feels like when it heals."

He closed the notebook and turned off the light.
Outside, a breeze stirred through the trees, carrying the faint scent of rain.
He imagined a pond somewhere — ripples still moving quietly, endlessly, unseen.

The first ripple is awareness.
The second is influence.
The third will be legacy.

Coach's Reflection – On Influence

"Stillness travels farther than sound."

Influence is not persuasion.
It is presence in motion.

You cannot force a ripple to spread.
You can only drop the stone —
and trust the water to remember.

True influence begins the moment you stop trying to convince.
It's not about power, position, or persuasion.
It's about the quiet energy that shifts a room without saying a word.

The way you breathe, the way you pause,
the way you look at someone and make them feel seen —
these are the real conversations that change people.

You do not need to lead loudly to lead deeply.
Still water carries reflection farther than waves ever could.

When a leader becomes grounded,
others borrow their calm.
When a coach becomes still,
others find clarity in that silence.

That is the paradox of influence:
the less you try to make an impact,
the deeper the impact becomes.

True influence isn't about being remembered.
It's about leaving others more in touch with themselves.

PART IV

TRANSFORMATION

When Presence Becomes Influence

"Growth is not upward, it's inward."

CHAPTER 9

THE COACH BECOMES THE COACHEE

THE CULTURE OF CONVERSATION

"When conversation becomes culture, leadership becomes invisible."

It began quietly — as all real change does.
No announcement. No memo. No new policy.
Just a feeling.

People noticed it first in Arun's floor meetings.
There was more laughter. Fewer rushed replies.
Deadlines were still met, but the air no longer carried the scent of fear.
Someone joked that their team room felt "lighter."

Then something unexpected happened: **other managers started visiting.**
At first, they came out of curiosity — wondering why Arun's team seemed calmer yet more productive.

But they left puzzled by what they saw — no new tools, no slogans, no reward systems. Just conversations — genuine, reflective, human.

The Curiosity

One afternoon, during a leadership lunch, Sanjay Rao mentioned it.
"What's happening in your team, Arun?" he asked, more curious than critical.
"People keep saying the energy is different."

Arun smiled. "We've started talking more. And listening better."

Sanjay chuckled. "That's it?"

"That's it," said Arun simply.

Sanjay shook his head, amused. "You make it sound like magic."

Arun replied, "It's not magic. It's permission."

The room fell silent.

The Invitation

A few weeks later, HR noticed the same trend.
Engagement scores in Arun's division had risen — quietly but consistently.
Priya Nair, the HR Director, called him in.

"What's your secret?" she asked, half-smiling.

"No secret," Arun said. "Just conversations that matter."

Priya leaned forward. "Could you show others how?"

He hesitated. He wasn't a trainer. He wasn't even sure how to explain what had happened.
But then he remembered Meera's words:

"When a ripple returns, it becomes a wave."

"Alright," he said. "Let's try something."

The First Circle

The following month, twelve managers gathered in a quiet conference room — a mix of skepticism and curiosity in the air.
Arun opened the session by saying,
"This isn't a workshop. It's a circle.
No presentations. No slides. Just conversations."

He shared his own story — the early discomfort, the resistance, the small experiments, the first ripple.
He spoke not like a teacher, but like a traveler describing the road.

At first, people nodded politely. Then, slowly, stories began to surface. One admitted, "I don't really listen — I'm always preparing my answer."
Another said, "I think my team fears me more than they trust me."

And as their words filled the room, something shifted.
No one was interrupted. No one was judged.
It was just… listening.

By the end of the session, no one looked at the clock.

The Ripples Multiply

Within weeks, similar circles began forming on other floors.
People called them *"reflection hours"* or *"listening labs."*
Teams began opening meetings with questions like,
"What do we need to understand before we decide?"
"What are we not saying that needs to be said?"

The language of leadership was changing.
It wasn't about control anymore.
It was about curiosity.

Even Sanjay, initially skeptical, found himself staying silent longer in meetings.
He noticed that when he didn't rush to fill the silence, people offered deeper insights.
He began to understand what Arun meant by "permission."

The Email

One evening, Arun received an email from Meera.

Arun,
I hear the ripples are expanding. Tell me — how does it feel to watch what you began move beyond your reach?
– Meera

He stared at the message for a long time before replying.

Meera,
It feels like watching a pond become a river. It's not mine anymore

— and that feels right.
– Arun

The Company Town Hall

Months later, at the annual town hall, Priya announced a new initiative:
"Conversations That Create Change."
A company-wide movement inspired by Arun's team — though he hadn't named it, planned it, or even expected it.

When his name was mentioned, he felt a strange humility — pride without possession.
He glanced at his team — Riya smiling proudly, Dev nodding quietly — and felt the quiet fullness of purpose.

He remembered Meera's first question:

"When did you last feel proud of your work?"

He smiled to himself. *Now,* he thought again. *Still now.*

The ripple had become a river.
And in that flow, everyone had become both student and teacher.

Meanwhile, Elsewhere

Meera was sitting by the same pond where it had all begun.
She watched a leaf fall into the water, sending soft ripples outward.
She thought of Arun, of his team, of all the unseen lives now touched by their conversations.

She whispered to the wind,

"And so the pond remembers the stone."

Culture doesn't change through policies or posters.
It changes when people begin to feel safe enough to speak — and be heard.

Coach's Reflection – On Culture

Culture is not a statement on a wall.
It is a conversation that never stops.

Every meeting, every silence, every sigh between words —
they are all threads weaving the invisible fabric of "how we live here."

You cannot design culture on a spreadsheet.
You can only create the conditions for it to breathe.

Culture grows where fear recedes.
It listens where hierarchy softens.
It strengthens when trust replaces control.

Most leaders try to build culture,
as if it were an external structure.
But culture is not built —
it is grown.

It is grown through presence.
Through the small, consistent acts of listening, acknowledging, and choosing clarity over comfort.

When a conversation becomes a habit,
and a habit becomes a heartbeat,
you no longer have to protect culture —
it protects you.

Culture isn't what people say when they're being watched.
It's what they whisper when they feel safe.

CHAPTER 10

THE TEST OF INTEGRITY

THE RIPPLE THAT HOLDS

"Integrity is not about what you stand for — it's about what you won't stand without."

The monsoon had returned.
Rain traced silver lines down the tall glass windows of Zenith Global's 18th floor. It blurred the city lights below.

Arun sat in the boardroom, a report open before him — numbers precise, projections polished. But something beneath the clean data was wrong.

He'd seen it three nights earlier — a quiet error in the new financial forecasts. Not intentional, but convenient.
It made their quarterly results look better than they were.

He had mentioned it to the finance team, who nodded vaguely, saying,
"Don't worry, sir — we'll fix it next quarter. Everyone's doing it."

It echoed in his mind like a small stone hitting still water.

But the sentence wouldn't leave him. *Everyone's doing it.*

It echoed in his mind like a small stone hitting still water.

The Review

The senior review was underway.
Sanjay Rao, his boss, led the discussion briskly. "This quarter looks clean," he said, scanning the slides. "Finally, some relief for the board."

Arun felt his chest tighten. He glanced at the slide again — the same one he knew wasn't entirely true.
His palms grew damp.

Sanjay turned to him. "Arun, you've really steadied the ship. Excellent work."

He hesitated. "Sir, about the numbers—"

Sanjay interrupted, "I know they're tight, but we'll balance it next quarter. Let's keep this clean for now. The board's watching."

He looked at Arun directly.
A subtle message. A test hidden behind professionalism.

Arun's old instincts flared — *don't make trouble, don't stand out, don't break the rhythm.*

But something deeper spoke louder this time — a still voice that had grown stronger through every conversation, every reflection, every pause.

He looked at the slide again.
Then at his team — Riya, Dev, others — watching silently, trusting him.

He thought of Meera's words:

"Conviction doesn't say, 'I'm right.'
It says, 'I'm clear.'"

He took a breath.
The room went quiet.

"Sir," he said softly but firmly, "these numbers aren't accurate. There's an over projection. We need to correct it before submission."

Sanjay's smile faded. "Arun, this isn't the time for idealism. The board meeting is tomorrow."

"With respect," Arun said, "it's exactly the time. If we speak of trust and culture, we can't build it on adjustment."

The silence deepened.

A few heads turned. Dev looked stunned. Riya's eyes widened — proud, scared, both.

Sanjay leaned back slowly. "You're aware this could delay the report? The board won't like it."

Arun met his gaze calmly. "Then we'll explain. With honesty."

For a long moment, no one spoke.
Then Sanjay sighed — a sound halfway between frustration and reluctant respect.
"Do what you need to," he said curtly. "But you'll own the decision."

"I already do," said Arun.

The Aftermath

The next day, the report was corrected.
The board meeting was tense but transparent.
There were questions, frowns, a few sharp remarks.

But no disaster followed.
Instead, something quiet yet extraordinary happened.

A week later, Sanjay stopped by Arun's office. He didn't sit.
He just said, "You were right to fix it."

Arun looked up, surprised.

Sanjay continued, softer now, "It's been years since someone said 'no' to me for the right reason. Don't lose that."

And he walked away.

The Ripple That Reached Back

That evening, Arun returned to his team.
They were working late, tired but upbeat.

Riya looked up. "Sir, we heard what happened,' Riya said softly. 'Thank you — for standing up.

He smiled faintly. “For what?”

“For all of us,” she said. “It made us believe this culture isn’t just talk.”

Dev added, with his usual dry humor, “You’ve officially ruined shortcuts for the rest of us.”

Laughter rippled across the room.
And in that laughter, Arun felt the weight of leadership transform into something lighter — responsibility held with grace.

He opened his notebook one last time that night and wrote:

“Integrity is the ripple that never fades.
It doesn’t make you popular. It makes you peaceful.”

Elsewhere

At home, Meera read the brief note he’d sent her:

“Faced resistance again. This time, I didn’t react. I responded.”

She smiled and whispered to herself,

“The pond has learned to hold its own ripples.”

Integrity isn’t the absence of temptation.

It’s the quiet decision to stay aligned, even when no one notices.

Coach's Reflection – On Integrity

Integrity is not about perfection.
It is about alignment.

It is the quiet agreement between your values and your actions —
between what you know to be right
and what you are willing to stand for.

Integrity rarely roars.
More often, it whispers,
"Stay true,"
even when that truth costs you comfort.

Many mistake integrity for morality —
as if it were a performance of virtue.
But integrity is not about appearing good;
it is about being whole.

To live with integrity is to move as one —
no separation between the voice inside and the words outside.

In the coaching space, I have seen leaders try to borrow
courage from their titles,
until life asks them to act from their truth instead.

That moment — when fear meets alignment —
is where transformation truly completes.

When you act with integrity,
you may lose applause,

but you gain peace.
And peace, unlike approval, does not expire.

Integrity is the ripple that travels quietly —
and never stops moving.

PART V

LEGACY

When Ripples Return

CHAPTER 11

THE RIPPLE RETURNS

"Every ripple that returns carries a lesson the stone never knew it taught."

Three years had passed.
The world outside had changed — new markets, new teams, new technologies — but inside Zenith Global, something deeper had shifted.
The culture that began as a whisper had become a hum.

People still spoke of efficiency, but now in the same breath as empathy.
Conversations that once started with "targets" now began with "what matters most."
Listening had become not a practice, but a presence.

And at the quiet center of it all, Arun had moved into a new role —
Head of Transformation.
A title that sounded big but, to him, simply meant *keeper of questions.*

The Invitation

It was a bright afternoon when Riya walked into his office, a file in her hand and a sparkle in her eyes.

"Sir, do you have a minute?" she asked.

"Always for you, Riya," he smiled.

She handed him a letter. "We've been invited to speak at the Global Leadership Forum — they want to hear about Zenith's 'Coaching Culture.'"

Arun raised his eyebrows. "Our what?"

Riya laughed. "That's what they're calling it now."

He leaned back, amused. "A few years ago, we were just trying to listen better."

"Exactly," she said. "And now it's a case study."

He smiled, proud but humbled. "Who'll present?"

She hesitated. "Actually… I was hoping to."

He nodded instantly. "You should."

Her face brightened. "Really?"

"Riya," he said softly, "you're the ripple. It's your turn to create your own circles."

She left the room with tears she didn't want him to see.

The Forum

A month later, Riya stood on a stage in front of hundreds of leaders from across industries.
Her hands trembled slightly as she began.

"Three years ago," she said, "our team was struggling. We had results, but no trust. Then something changed — not through a program, but through a person who started listening differently."

She shared stories — of the pilot, the reflection circles, the meetings that became conversations.
She didn't use the word *coaching* often. She used the word *listening*.

By the end of her talk, the room was silent — the kind of silence that listens.
She finished with a sentence that made Arun, sitting in the audience, smile quietly.

"We discovered that leadership is not about being followed — it's about creating more leaders who listen."

The applause was warm, genuine.
But what moved Arun most wasn't the applause.
It was the look in Riya's eyes — calm, steady, clear.
The same stillness Meera once mirrored for him.

After the Event

Later that evening, as the crowd dispersed, Riya found Arun standing by the glass railing overlooking the city lights.

"You were right," she said. "Ripples really do return."

He smiled. "They always do. Just never in the way we expect."

She hesitated, then added, "I've been thinking… maybe it's time I start coaching too."

Arun nodded. "You already have."

They stood together in silence, watching the city glow beneath them — alive with unspoken stories, unseen ripples.

Elsewhere

Far away, Meera sat on a wooden bench near the same pond where everything had begun.
The air was cool, the water still.
She was older now — slower, gentler — but her eyes still carried that quiet depth.

She had heard about Zenith's transformation through a colleague.
She didn't seek recognition; she never had.
But knowing the ripple had reached so far filled her with quiet joy.

She picked up a small stone and dropped it gently into the pond.
Ripples spread outward, touching everything, returning softly to the edges.

She whispered,

"The stone never sees the end of its ripple."

And smiled.

Back at Zenith

In his office, Arun closed his laptop after reading Riya's post-event note:

"You once told me to listen without an agenda. I finally understand what you meant. It's not just a skill — it's a way of being."

He smiled and wrote a single reply:

"And that's how the next ripple begins."

He turned off the lights, stepped out, and for the first time in years, didn't look back to check the office.
He didn't need to.
It was moving on its own.

When transformation is real, it no longer belongs to the one who began it.
It belongs to everyone who carries it forward — and to the silence that holds them all.

Coach's Reflection – On Legacy

Legacy is not what you leave behind.
It is what continues because you let go.

We often think of legacy as monuments, memories, or milestones —
something others remember us by.
But the real legacy is quieter.
It doesn't need credit, or nameplates, or applause.

Legacy lives in behaviors —
in the questions people keep asking,
the pauses they start honoring,
the gentleness they begin to show without knowing where it came from.

You know your work has found its way when your language becomes another's instinct.
When your values echo in voices you've never met.
When what you once guided is now guiding itself.

The most beautiful legacy of coaching —
and of leadership —
is the moment you become unnecessary.

It's when the ripples move without you.
When the pond no longer waits for your stone.
When others begin creating their own circles in still water.

That is the quiet completion of purpose.
Not the end — just the surrender.

Legacy is not remembered by name.
It's remembered by the stillness it leaves behind.

CHAPTER 12

THE SILENCE BETWEEN WORDS

The morning light was soft — that gentle kind of gold that doesn't fall but lingers.
Meera sat on the veranda of her small home on the outskirts of the city, surrounded by books, plants, and silence that had shape.

Her coaching calendar was nearly empty now.
She had started saying no to new clients, not out of fatigue, but out of fullness.
She no longer needed to fill her days with conversations; she was learning to listen to life itself.

In front of her sat her old leather notebook — the same one from years ago, worn at the corners, its pages filled with questions, reflections, and ripples of her journey.
On today's page, she had written just one sentence:

"Where does listening end, and life begin?"

She smiled faintly. The question didn't need an answer. It only needed attention.

The Visit

That afternoon, a young woman arrived — a new coach in training, wide-eyed and earnest.
"Ms. Anand," she said nervously, "I've read about your work with Zenith Global. You transformed their culture completely. How did you do it?"

Meera smiled. "I didn't."

The woman looked confused. "But everyone says—"

"I asked questions," Meera said simply. "And then I got out of the way."

The young woman frowned. "But surely you had a plan, a process?"

Meera nodded toward the pond outside her window. "Do you see that water?"

The woman looked. The surface was perfectly still.

"When the pond is still," Meera said, "it reflects everything clearly.
But the moment it tries to control the reflection, it loses it."

The woman was silent, thinking.

"So your method," she said softly, "was stillness?"

Meera smiled. "Presence. Stillness is not the absence of sound — it's the fullness of attention."

The Letter

Later that evening, Meera opened her inbox.
A new message from Arun.

Meera,
It's been years since our first session, and yet your questions still guide me. I wanted to tell you — Riya now leads the 'Ripple Project' across our global offices. She's training others to coach. The pond has become an ocean.
Thank you — for starting something you never claimed to own.
With gratitude,
Arun

Meera's eyes softened.
She closed her laptop and looked out at the twilight sky.

The first star had appeared — faint, patient, timeless.
She whispered, "Every ripple finds its sea."

The Conversation That Needed No Words

The next morning, she visited the pond.
The same one from the beginning of the story — still, eternal, unchanged.
She sat on the same rock, held a smooth stone in her palm, and for a long time, didn't move.

The air was cool. The breeze was gentle.
She could almost hear the echoes of her own journey —
the voices of leaders who had once come to her heavy with questions, now lighter with clarity.

Finally, she dropped the stone.
It sank quietly.
The ripples spread — soft, steady, endless.

She closed her eyes and felt a deep peace wash over her.
She realized something simple yet profound:

"The work was never about changing others.
It was about remembering stillness — and letting others see themselves in it."

When the coach becomes the listener of life itself,
the ripples no longer need guidance — they know their way.

CHAPTER 13

THE MIRROR RETURNS

The day was unusually still — not quiet, but *expectant.*
Even the trees outside Meera's window seemed to be holding their breath.

She was sitting at her desk, preparing notes for what might be her last public talk —
a keynote for a gathering of coaches titled *"The Art of Letting Go."*

She had spoken on that theme many times.
But today, as she reread her draft, something in her felt different — almost uncertain.

Her words looked wise, but distant.
As if written by someone who used to know her.

For the first time in years, Meera felt a strange emptiness.
Not doubt, exactly — but a quiet question pressing against her chest:

"Have I really let go?"

The Call

Her phone buzzed.
A message from Arun.

*"In your city today for meetings.
If you're free, can I stop by?"*

She smiled. *How fitting,* she thought.
The ripple was coming home.

When he arrived that evening, the air carried the faint scent of rain.
Arun looked older — softer, grounded — the kind of presence that didn't need to fill space anymore.

"Coach," he said warmly, "it's been too long."

She smiled. "You're one of the few who still call me that."

"Always will," he said, settling into the chair opposite hers.

The Conversation

They spoke for hours — about work, about Riya, about how listening had become a company language.
But as the evening deepened, Arun noticed something in her tone — a pause too long, a sigh too soft.

He leaned forward. "Are *you* okay, Meera?"

She hesitated. "I'm fine," she said automatically, then caught herself.
Old habits die quietly.

After a long silence, she admitted, "Lately, I've been wondering if I've really lived what I've taught — letting go, staying curious, trusting the flow."

Arun smiled gently. "Even the calmest pond has currents beneath."

She looked at him, amused. "Quoting metaphors back at me now?"

"Learned from the best," he said.
Then, more softly, "You don't have to hold the ripple anymore. It's moving on its own."

Meera's eyes glistened. "I know. But part of me misses being part of it."

He nodded. "I understand. But maybe that's the next lesson — to trust that the water remembers even when the stone is gone."

She exhaled slowly.
There it was — the reflection she needed, offered by the very student who had once sat across from her, lost and defensive.

He was now holding the stillness for her.

The Mirror Moment

After a while, they stepped outside.
The sky had turned indigo. Crickets sang softly in the background.
They stood by the pond together — the same pond that had begun it all.

"Do you remember the first question you asked me?" Arun said.

Meera smiled faintly. "When did you last feel proud of your work?"

"Yes," he said. "I never answered it then. But if you asked me now…"
He paused. "I'd say — today."

She turned to him, surprised. "Today?"

He nodded. "Because today, I got to remind *you* what you once reminded me."

Her laughter broke softly into the night air.
Tears welled, but they weren't of sadness. They were of completion.

They stood in silence, watching the moonlight touch the surface of the water.
The ripples were faint but endless — quiet proof that movement doesn't need to be seen to exist.

Meera spoke softly, almost to herself:

"Perhaps this is what mastery really is — not knowing more, but needing less."

Arun nodded. "And remembering that even coaches need to be coached — by life, by others, by silence."

They both smiled.

In that shared stillness, the circle closed — not as an ending, but as a quiet return.

When the teacher becomes the student, wisdom becomes whole.
When the listener is listened to, silence learns to speak again.

"The mirror doesn't keep what it reflects.
It only reminds the light where it came from."

CHAPTER 14

THE POND REMEMBERS

The morning sky over Singapore was painted with light — a gradient of silver and rose.
Inside a glass tower overlooking the Marina, Riya Kapoor stood before a room of thirty young leaders from across the world.

The placard on the table read:
"The Ripple Project – Global Chapter Launch."

She looked out at the faces — eager, anxious, curious — and felt a strange mix of pride and humility.
This wasn't just another corporate initiative.
It was a continuation — a living echo of something that began years ago, in a quiet conversation between a coach and a leader who had learned to listen.

The Opening

"Welcome," she began, her voice calm, assured.
"When I was an intern, my boss once did something unusual.
He listened — really listened.
That moment changed how I saw leadership forever."

She paused, letting the silence breathe.

"This project isn't about training. It's about remembering. Remembering that the simplest human acts — listening, trusting, pausing — create the most extraordinary impact."

She looked down briefly at her notes.
In the corner of the page, she had written a small quote from Meera's journal, one she had found in Arun's files years ago:

'Every ripple carries the memory of the stone that began it.'

She read it aloud.
And for a moment, the room grew still — as if the air itself were listening.

The Conversation That Followed

During a group dialogue, one of the young leaders — a woman from Manila — asked,
"How do we keep a culture like this alive? How do we stop it from becoming another management fad?"

Riya smiled gently.
"By not owning it," she said. "By letting it belong to everyone."

The woman nodded slowly, understanding.
In that instant, Riya saw herself — years ago — asking Meera the same kind of question with the same uncertainty.

And she realized: she wasn't passing on a program.
She was passing on a *way of seeing.*

Later That Evening

After the session, Riya sat alone on the terrace of the building, watching the harbor lights shimmer across the water.
She opened her notebook — not a laptop, not a tablet — a real notebook, as both Arun and Meera had taught her.

She wrote:

"I used to think coaching was about helping people grow.
Now I know it's about remembering what's already whole."

She looked at the skyline, its reflection rippling softly in the bay, and smiled.

"Maybe water is just life reminding us to keep moving."

A soft breeze brushed her face, carrying the scent of the sea.

She whispered quietly to no one in particular,

"Thank you, Meera. Thank you, Arun."

And somewhere — across time, distance, and silence — the ripples heard her.

Elsewhere

In another part of the world, Arun was preparing to retire.
His farewell speech was brief, simple — just as he had lived his leadership.

"I've learned," he said, "that success is not the height you reach but the depth you touch.
If I've done anything right, it's because someone once listened to

me until I found my own voice.
So, if you remember one thing — let it be this: listen as if the world depends on it.
Because it does."

When the applause faded, he looked out across the audience and saw faces — Dev, Riya, and others — each one carrying their own ripples now.
He felt no need to say more.

And at the Pond

That evening, Meera returned to her quiet pond for the last time that season.
The air was cool, the water like glass.
She dropped a small pebble into the center — her old ritual — and watched the ripples move outward, slow and steady.

As the circles expanded, they caught the reflection of the sky — pink, blue, and gold.
She smiled, remembering every voice, every silence, every unseen ripple that had ever begun from this still place.

A whisper rose in her mind, light as a sigh:

"The pond remembers."

And in that moment, she knew — she had not changed the world.
She had simply reminded it to listen.

Legacy is not a monument built in our name.
It is the quiet continuity of what we once made possible.

Every coach is a stone.
Every conversation, a ripple.
Every listener, a pond remembering itself.

EPILOGUE – THE STILL WATER

Where the story rests, and the listening begins.

"At the end of every ripple, there is silence —
and in that silence, the next ripple waits."

The morning was pale and soundless.
Mist hovered above the pond like a thought not yet spoken.
Arun stood by the water's edge, hands in his pockets, watching how the light played with the ripples.

It had been months since Meera's last session with him.
The rhythm of work had returned — the meetings, the strategies, the travel.
But something in him had changed.
Not loudly, not visibly — but like water remembering the shape of a stone that once entered it.

He no longer rushed to answer.
He noticed the spaces between words.
He began to sense when his team's silence was not disengagement, but thought.
And every time he caught himself about to react, he heard Meera's voice in memory:

"Pause. The pond will tell you what's next."

That morning, he realized he hadn't come here for closure.
He had come because the stillness felt like company.

He crouched down and picked up a small, flat stone.
Its surface was cool, smooth, ordinary.

He remembered how Meera had once described coaching as *"the art of throwing a stone with awareness."*

"You can't control the ripples," she had said.
"But you can choose how gently the stone enters."

He smiled. She had been right about more than that.

He tossed the stone lightly into the water.
It landed with a quiet *plunk* — no splash, just movement.
The circles spread, widening softly, until they touched the reeds at the edges and disappeared.

The surface grew calm again — but not empty.
The water held the memory of motion.

For the first time, Arun understood what Meera had truly been teaching him.
It was never about performance or persuasion.
It was about presence — the kind that asks for nothing, yet changes everything.

He looked around the pond.
Somewhere in the distance, a bird lifted off, wings catching the

faint light.
He could feel the morning opening — slow, deliberate.

He thought of the people he coached now:
the young manager who was afraid of failing,
the quiet woman who didn't believe her voice mattered,
the restless executive chasing impossible targets.

In each of them, he saw a reflection of his earlier self — anxious, certain, always running.

He had no grand wisdom to give them.
Just attention.
Just presence.
And that seemed to be enough.

As he turned to leave, Arun glanced one last time at the pond.
The surface was still again.
Only faint concentric circles lingered for a moment before dissolving.

It struck him that this was how change really happened —
not as noise or revolution, but as gentle continuity.

Every conversation, every pause, every act of listening
created motion beyond what anyone could measure.

The ripples might fade, but the water was never the same.

He whispered into the quiet air:

"Thank you."

The wind shifted.
The pond shimmered.
And the silence — listening as always — answered back.

PART VI

THE LIVING RIPPLES

CHAPTER 15

THE RIPPLE FRAMEWORK

THE FIVE LEVELS OF PRESENCE: HOW AWARENESS BECOMES STILLNESS

"The pond doesn't teach the stone how to fall; it teaches everything else how to receive."

Leadership is less about direction and more about *resonance*. When a leader is present, others align—not because they must, but because they can finally feel safe enough to breathe.

In coaching, this resonance unfolds in layers—like ripples that move outward from a single drop of awareness.
Each ripple represents a level of presence, and every level deepens the conversation between the self and the world.

Ripple 1 – Awareness: Noticing Without Judgment

Arun once described his early meetings as *battles for space*.
He would fill every silence with data, direction, or reassurance.
When Meera first asked him to *"listen to the room without fixing*

it," he thought she meant silence.
She meant something deeper—*awareness.*

Awareness begins before listening; it is noticing *how you are showing up.*
It's the pause between the email you just sent and the meeting you're about to start.
It's the quiet internal check: *Am I here, or still in the last conversation?*

Reflection:
Awareness isn't control.
It's consent—to meet this moment exactly as it is.

Practice — The Two-Minute Arrival
Before any key conversation, close your eyes for two minutes.
Breathe in for four counts, out for six.
Ask silently:

- *What emotion is present in me right now?*
- *What might the other person be carrying?*
  Do nothing with the answers.
  Just know them.

Ripple 2 – Listening: Holding the Silence Open

When Meera coached senior executives, she often began with this sentence:

"Tell me what you're not saying."

At first, the question startled them.
Then the silence stretched—and something real emerged.

Listening is not waiting to reply; it's creating a container large enough for truth.
In organizations, leaders often mistake activity for connection.
But people don't need more talking—they need to be *heard into clarity*.

Reflection:
Listening is how we lend dignity to another's experience.
It is the most economical form of leadership.

Practice — The Three-Second Rule
In your next meeting, wait three full seconds after someone finishes speaking.
Resist the urge to answer or summarize.
Notice what additional insight—or courage—emerges in that pause.

Leadership Insight
Teams mirror their leader's pace.
When you slow down to listen, you recalibrate the organization's nervous system.

Ripple 3 – Trust : Letting Go of Control

In a coaching circle at Zenith Global, a manager once asked,

"If I stop directing, how do I make sure things don't fall apart?"

Meera smiled. "They might—for a moment. Then they'll find their own balance."

Trust is the willingness to release control long enough for others to rise.
It is not blind optimism; it's confident humility.
When leaders create safety, initiative replaces obedience.

Reflection:
Trust grows in the soil of transparency.
You cannot demand it—you can only demonstrate it.

Practice — The Trust Transfer

1. Choose one decision you usually make alone.
2. Invite a team member to lead it.
3. Offer boundaries but no blueprint.
4. When anxiety arises, breathe instead of intervening.

Coaching Insight
A coachee's first breakthrough often comes when the coach trusts their silence enough not to *rescue them.*
The same is true for leadership.

Ripple 4 – Integrity: Alignment in Action

Integrity is not a rulebook; it's resonance between inner truth and outer choice.
For Arun, the test came when profit targets clashed with his team's well-being.
He paused, revisited his values, and said, *"We'll deliver differently, but not dishonestly."*
That sentence changed the meeting—and the culture.

Integrity is felt before it's seen.
People may not always agree with your decision, but they will sense when it's grounded.

Reflection:
Integrity is not moral posturing; it's coherence.
It's the calm in your tone when your principles and actions are in tune.

Practice — The Alignment Audit
At week's end, journal three moments when you felt "off."
Ask:

- *What value was compromised?*
- *What would alignment have looked like?*
  Write a one-line intention to correct the drift next week.

Leadership Insight
Integrity is contagious.
It frees others from pretending.

Ripple 5 – Stillness: Presence as Legacy

In her final session with Arun, Meera said,

"Stillness isn't the absence of sound; it's the presence of understanding."

Stillness is what remains when you no longer need to perform.
It is leadership beyond effort—the moment when influence flows through, not from, you.

In coaching, stillness is the sacred interval after a client's insight—
the space where transformation settles into being.
In organizations, it appears as calm clarity amid change.

Reflection:
Stillness is not withdrawal; it's completion.

Practice — The One-Minute Stillpoint
At day's end, close all screens.
Sit upright, eyes soft.
For one minute, do nothing.
Let the day's ripples return to still water.
End with this quiet affirmation:

"I have done enough for now."

Integrating the Five Ripples

Ripple	Essence	Question to Hold
Awareness	Noticing self	"What am I bringing?"
Listening	Receiving others	"What wants to be heard?"
Trust	Releasing control	"What can I let unfold?"
Integrity	Acting in alignment	"What choice honors my truth?"
Stillness	Being whole	"What remains when I stop trying?"

When all five ripples coexist, a leader no longer manages energy—they become it.

Closing Meditation — The Circle Returns

Sit quietly for five breaths.
Imagine a single ripple expanding from your center—awareness, listening, trust, integrity, stillness—each circle larger but lighter.
When the last ripple reaches the edge of the pond, picture it returning toward you.
This is the reminder:

Everything you give through presence returns as peace.

CHAPTER 16

THE POND WITHIN

PRACTICES FOR INNER CLARITY AND RENEWAL

***"The pond does not chase reflection;
it receives it."***

The following practices emerged from conversations that once began as stories. They are not methods to master, but mirrors to remember yourself through.

Inside every leader, every coach, every human being, there is a pond.
Some days it's stirred by deadlines, noise, and endless motion.
Other days it settles — and in that still water, truth becomes visible.

These practices are invitations to return to that inner pond.
They are simple, portable, and human — meant for offices, corridors, screens, and silent mornings alike.
Each begins with awareness, flows through experience, and settles into quiet action.

---

1. The Three-Breath Reset

"Before you speak, arrive."

When Arun began coaching his leadership team, he noticed meetings opened with tension — people spoke fast, defensive, impatient.
Meera suggested one tiny ritual: three conscious breaths before any discussion.

At first, they laughed. "We don't have time for yoga," someone said.
A month later, the same group began meetings by closing their eyes for ten seconds — one inhale to arrive, one exhale to release, one breath to listen.
Arguments softened. Ideas flowed. The tone shifted — invisibly, yet unmistakably.

Practice Steps

1. **Arrive** – One slow inhale. Feel your feet on the ground.
2. **Release** – Exhale through the mouth, letting go of the last task.
3. **Receive** – Breathe in again, gently, as if welcoming this exact moment.

Use it before a call, presentation, or difficult conversation.
It resets not the situation, but *your nervous system.*

Three breaths can reopen a day that felt closed.

---

2. The Mirror Moment

"Awareness begins when reflection replaces reaction."

In coaching supervision, Meera often asked,

"What part of you showed up in that session?"

It was not criticism; it was curiosity.
Awareness of self transforms the quality of connection.

Riya, now leading global coaching programs, used the same question after a team disagreement.
Instead of blaming, she paused and said aloud,

"Maybe my need to be right just entered the room."
The tension dissolved. The team smiled. The conversation reset.

Practice Steps

1. After any emotionally charged moment, take thirty seconds alone.
2. Ask, *"Which version of me just spoke?"*
3. Note it — not to judge, but to understand.
4. Later, reflect: *What would my grounded self have said instead?*

This practice builds emotional literacy — the leader's quiet radar.

The mirror is not for vanity; it is for clarity.

---

3. The Listening Pause

"Silence is the bridge between two truths."

During a strategy meeting, Dev — once the skeptic — tried something new.
When his colleague finished an idea, he waited three seconds before replying.
At first, the room felt awkward.
Then, others began to think before speaking.
Within minutes, the discussion deepened; voices softened.
The meeting ended early — not because they rushed, but because they finally *heard* each other.

Practice Steps

1. In your next conversation, delay your response by three seconds.
2. During that pause, notice the other person's expression and your impulse.
3. Let curiosity replace reaction.
4. When you do speak, use the phrase: "I'm thinking aloud — tell me what lands for you."

Why it works
Silence signals respect.
In coaching, it allows insight to surface.
In leadership, it gives permission for authenticity.

The pause is not empty; it's full of what matters.

---

4. The Ripple Journal

"Every day leaves circles behind — notice them."

Meera kept a small notebook titled *Ripples.*
Each evening, she wrote two short lines:

What ripple did I create today?
What ripple did I inherit and continue?

No paragraphs. No analysis. Just two sentences of awareness.

When Arun began the same habit, he discovered patterns — which meetings lifted him, which drained him, which words encouraged growth.
Awareness turned into conscious design.

Practice Steps

1. Keep a small notebook or digital note titled *Ripples.*
2. At day's end, complete the two prompts above.
3. Once a week, read your entries in silence.
4. Circle one pattern you wish to reinforce, and one you wish to release.

Leadership Application

Use this journal in team reflections.
Ask members to share one positive ripple they've observed from someone else that week.
It builds gratitude, trust, and cross-awareness.

A culture of reflection is built one small note at a time.

---

5. The Two-Chair Dialogue

"Sometimes clarity needs a change of seat."

In coaching, when clients were stuck between choices, Meera used a simple physical metaphor.
She placed two chairs facing each other and said,

"Sit in the first as yourself today. Speak your fear."
"Now move to the second — speak as your wiser self a year from now."

The shift was immediate.
Changing seats changed perspective.
The future self always knew what the present self doubted.

Practice Steps

1. Place two chairs (or imagine them).
2. In the first, voice your current worry or decision.
3. Move to the second. Breathe. Speak as your wiser future self responding.
4. Note the difference in tone and energy.
5. Return to the first seat and write one line beginning with, *"I realize now that…"*

For Teams

Use a metaphorical version: assign "current reality" and "desired state" chairs during retrospectives.
It externalizes dialogue and invites empathy.

Wisdom often arrives when the body moves.

---

6. The Silent Close

"The meeting is not over until awareness arrives."

After every leadership retreat, Meera ended with five minutes of silence.
No wrap-up slides, no next steps — just breathing together.
The first few times, participants fidgeted.
By the third retreat, no one moved.
They understood: silence was not absence; it was *integration*.

Practice Steps

1. End meetings with a one-minute silent reflection.
2. Invite everyone to note:
   - One insight
   - One appreciation
   - One next step
3. After a minute, allow anyone who wishes to share.

Why it matters
Without silence, learning leaks.
Stillness lets meaning settle — turning discussion into a decision.

The quiet after the conversation is where understanding takes root.

---

7. The One-Line Intention

"What you name, you nurture."

Riya began each Monday asking her team for one line:

"What intention will guide you this week?"
Responses varied — "Clarity over speed." "Listen more." "Trust before talking."
They pinned those lines near their desks.
By Friday, every action seemed to echo them.

Practice Steps

1. Choose one guiding word or phrase each week. (e.g., "Presence," "Patience," "Curiosity.")
2. Write it where you'll see it often.
3. At week's end, ask: *Did this word shape my behavior?*

Leadership Application
Use it in team check-ins.
It aligns energy without a heavy process.

An intention is a quiet compass.

---

8. The Gratitude Ripple

"Recognition completes the circle."

Late in his career, Arun began a ritual he called "The Circle of Thanks."
Every Friday, he sent three short messages of appreciation — no template, no formality.
Within weeks, others started doing the same.
Performance conversations grew kinder, feedback became real, and motivation stopped needing reminders.

Practice Steps

1. Each week, thank three people — specifically and sincerely.
2. Express what you *noticed*, not just what you *liked.*
3. Don't expect replies; gratitude is its own closure.

Coaching Insight

Acknowledgment is a form of witnessing.
When people feel seen, they listen differently.

The ripple of gratitude returns as trust.

Bringing It Together

These eight practices are not tasks to complete; they are invitations to remember.
The goal is not mastery but consistency.
The pond inside you clears through repetition — small acts done consciously.

If you practice even one daily, you'll notice:

- Conversations slow down, but progress accelerates.
- Decisions become cleaner.
- Relationships breathe again.

The leader becomes lighter.
The coach becomes quieter.
And through them both, presence becomes culture.

When the pond within is clear, the ripples outside take care of themselves.

CHAPTER 17

CONVERSATIONS THAT CREATE CHANGE

A FIELD GUIDE FOR COACHES AND LEADERS WHO LISTEN

"Every coaching conversation is a mirror—
not for the coach to see the client,
but for the client to see themselves more clearly."

Great coaching is not about fixing or guiding.
It is about evoking — inviting truth to rise naturally, like ripples on still water.

Each of the following conversations is a circle of its own: delicate, deliberate, and deeply human.

---

1. The Conversation of Permission

"Transformation begins when someone feels safe enough to be seen."

The Story

A new client once entered Meera's room with arms crossed, eyes guarded.
"Let's just get to the tools," she said.
Meera smiled and asked gently,

"Before tools — may I ask what kind of space you need today?"

That simple invitation softened her posture.
The work began — not with insight, but with permission.

The Insight

Before a client can open, they must know their truth will survive the room.
Safety is not a policy — it is presence without judgment.

The Practice

1. Begin each session by asking: "What would make this space useful to you today?"
2. Reflect back what you hear — tone, pace, mood.
3. Maintain soft eye contact and relaxed stillness for the first thirty seconds after they speak; let them feel held.
4. End the session by checking: "Did you get what you needed from this conversation?"

Permission is not granted once — it is renewed in every breath.

💧 2. The Conversation of Truth

"When the story is told honestly, it starts to dissolve."

The Story

A senior leader came to coaching, certain that burnout was "just workload."
As he spoke, Meera noticed his voice tighten whenever he mentioned his father's expectations.
She leaned in and said softly,

"You speak of deadlines, but I hear duty. Which one drains you more?"
He went silent, then whispered, "Duty."
That was the doorway.

The Insight

Truth hides in repetition.
A coach's task is to listen beneath content — to emotion, to the word that trembles.

The Practice

1. When patterns appear, mirror them neutrally: "I notice this word keeps returning…"
2. Ask, "What makes that word important right now?"
3. Let silence do the work; truth rarely enters under pressure.
4. When the client names their truth, acknowledge it simply: "That sounds significant."

Truth does not need approval; it needs a witness.

◇ 3. The Conversation of Choice

"Freedom is not found in options, but in ownership."

The Story

A client once said, "I don't have a choice — I have to stay."
Meera placed a pebble in her palm and said,

"You may choose to hold or release it. Either way, it's still your hand."
He laughed, then sighed.
"I suppose staying is also a choice."
That awareness shifted everything.

The Insight

Victimhood ends where agency begins.
Coaching reawakens the client's authorship of their own story.

The Practice

1. When you hear "I have to," ask, "What would happen if you didn't?"
2. Help the client list choices they do have, even uncomfortable ones.
3. Encourage responsibility, not reassurance.
4. Close by asking, "What choice aligns with who you want to become?"

Choice is the hinge between awareness and action.

◈ 4. The Conversation of Shadow

"What we resist owns us until we name it."

The Story

A confident executive avoided feedback about impatience.

When Meera asked, "What emotion do you feel just before you interrupt someone?"
He paused, startled.
"Fear," he said. "Fear they'll waste time."
Seeing his shadow — fear disguised as efficiency — opened compassion, not shame.
Change followed quietly.

The Insight
Every strength has a shadow; every shadow hides a gift.
Coaching helps the client befriend both.

The Practice

1. Notice recurring frustrations or defenses — invite curiosity, not correction.
2. Ask: "If this reaction had a message, what would it be?"
3. Encourage the client to thank the shadow for its original purpose.
4. Ask: "What might this energy look like when expressed wisely?"

Integration is gentler than elimination.

---

5. The Conversation of Vision

"The future speaks in whispers; listening makes it louder."

The Story
Riya once coached a young manager who couldn't see beyond quarterly targets.
"Imagine it's five years later," she said.

"What will make you proud, not just successful?"
He described mentoring others, creating calm spaces, having time to play music again.
Tears rolled down unnoticed.
A vision had spoken.

The Insight
Vision is not goal-setting — it is remembering what matters most.
Coaches evoke it through quiet curiosity, not frameworks.

The Practice

1. Ask future-self questions: "What will fulfillment feel like?"
2. Explore sensory details — sound, texture, light — to make vision real.
3. Anchor insight into present action: "What one small step today moves you toward that?"
4. Revisit the vision at the close of each session; let it mature.

The clearer the inner picture, the softer the outer striving.

🌙 6. The Conversation of Stillness

"When words end, knowing begins."

The Story
Toward the end of a long coaching journey, Meera and Arun often sat without talking.
Sometimes ten minutes passed in silence — no tension, no need.
One day, Arun smiled and said,

"I think I finally understand what you meant by presence."
Meera replied,
"And you didn't need my words to get there."

The Insight

Stillness is not a closing; it's absorption.
The coach withdraws so awareness can settle.

The Practice

1. When an insight lands, resist the urge to summarize.
2. Hold silence; let emotion and meaning merge.
3. Ask softly, "What is happening inside you right now?"
4. End with gratitude, not instruction.

Silence completes what speech begins.

◈ Bringing the Conversations Together

Each of these six conversations mirrors the five ripples of presence:

Ripple	Conversation	Essence
Awareness	Permission	Creating safe reflection
Listening	Truth	Hearing beneath words
Trust	Choice	Returning ownership
Integrity	Shadow	Integrating the whole self
Stillness	Vision / Silence	Allowing purpose to unfold

You do not need to master them sequentially.
They will appear naturally as your own presence deepens.

Some days you'll notice you are holding permission; other days, stillness.
All are simply expressions of awareness.

Coaching is not a method — it is a series of sacred conversations
that remind people who they already are.

CHAPTER 18

LEGACY RIPPLES IN REAL LIFE

Where the Water Carries the Learning Onward

"The pond never keeps a single ripple.
It simply passes each one forward."

Years had passed since Meera's first sessions with Arun.
Her teachings, once confined to quiet rooms, had begun to echo through others — coaches, leaders, teachers, and healers — each carrying a fragment of her stillness into new waters.
What began as one stone had become a living current.

Riya – The Circle Returns

The conference room at Zenith Global looked different now. Once a space of sharp corners and tighter schedules, it had become a circle — literally. Riya had replaced the boardroom table with a ring of simple chairs.

That morning, she welcomed twelve new managers into the *Listening Lab.*

No slides, no introductions. Just silence for the first sixty seconds.
Some shuffled awkwardly; others glanced at the clock.

Then Riya spoke:

"What if our first act of leadership is listening?"

By noon, the laughter was easier, and honesty had found its way back into the room.

Later that evening, she sent Meera a note:

We didn't train them today. We remembered together.

Legacy Reflection

Every time a leader sits in a circle instead of a hierarchy, a ripple returns home.

💧 Ananya – The Listening Classroom

Ananya taught literature at a public school on the outskirts of Mumbai.
She had once attended a short coaching workshop Riya facilitated — and had left with one phrase lodged in her mind:

"Presence changes learning."

She began experimenting.

Before each class, she invited her students to take one quiet breath together.
At first, the teenagers giggled; then they began to look forward to it.

When a shy student struggled to read aloud, Ananya paused beside her and whispered,

"Take your time. I'm listening."

The girl finished the paragraph without faltering.

That day, Ananya wrote in her journal:

Listening is not a method; it's a form of love.

A year later, her classroom won an innovation award — not for technology, but for empathy in education.

Legacy Reflection

When a teacher listens differently, learning itself begins to breathe.

◈ Omar – Stillness in the ICU

Dr. Omar was a senior physician in a busy metropolitan hospital.
He had never met Meera, but he had once heard her speak on a podcast about "the power of the pause."
He remembered the line:

"Stillness is not inaction. It is attention without panic."

Months later, during a night shift, a young nurse made a small error that nearly cost a life.
Her hands trembled as she stood before him.

Omar felt his own pulse quicken — anger, fear, exhaustion — and then he caught the phrase in his mind: *the pause.*

He took one breath, then another.
When he spoke, his tone was calm.
Together, they reviewed what happened.

The nurse began to cry, not out of guilt but relief.
At the end of the shift, she said,

"Thank you for listening instead of shouting."

Omar realized he had just practiced coaching without calling it that.

Legacy Reflection

Stillness in one heartbeat can steady an entire room.

◈ Dev – The Founder Who Learned to Pause

Dev had built a start-up from nothing — and nearly burned out keeping it alive.
After his coaching journey with Meera, he promised himself one thing: *never to confuse urgency with importance.*

Years later, when investors demanded faster returns, he gathered his team and said,

"We will grow at the speed of integrity."

Some left; most stayed.
The company didn't scale overnight — but it endured, profitable and peaceful.

Every Monday morning, before diving into targets, Dev began with five minutes of silence.

A new intern once asked why.
He smiled:

"Because silence reminds us who we work for — the work itself."

Legacy Reflection

In a noisy world, the leader who pauses becomes the compass.

Closing Reflection – The Water Remembers

Across continents and professions, Meera's ripple continued — through people she never met and moments she would never know.
None carried her name; all carried her essence.

In coaching, this is the truest legacy:

to touch others so quietly that they forget who started the movement,
and remember only what it felt like to be seen.

The pond never holds the ripple —
yet every ripple remembers the pond.

PART VII

CLOSING THE CIRCLE

Coach's Reflection – On Continuity

Continuity is not repetition.
It is remembrance in motion.

Every pause, every word, every act of awareness
leaves a trace — not to be preserved,
but to be passed on.

The work of a coach, a leader, or a listener
is not to hold the ripple in place,
but to trust that the water remembers.

Continuity is how wisdom travels —
not through instruction,
but through imitation of stillness.

You cannot own it,
you can only embody it,
until someone else begins to breathe the same quiet rhythm.

Then, without fanfare,
the circle continues —
teacher becoming student,
listener becoming voice,
presence becoming culture.

And when your part is done,
you realize something simple yet infinite:
the pond was never yours,
only your reflection was.

Continuity is not the ripple that endures —
it is the silence that allows the next one to begin.

AFTERWORD

A Letter to the Next Ripple

From one quiet presence to another.

"When the ripple reaches the shore, it doesn't stop—it becomes part of the tide."

Dear Reader,

If you've reached these pages, you have already created a ripple.
Every moment of attention you've given was an act of presence
—
and presence, like water, never goes to waste.

I began this story as a meditation on listening.
But as I wrote, I realized it was also about memory —
how the world remembers us not through titles or triumphs,
but through the calm we leave behind in others.

The world you return to after this book will still be loud, fast, and certain.
But inside you, there is now a pond —
clear enough to reflect what truly matters.
You may not always feel it, yet it is there: waiting, patient, steady.

If you ever doubt the value of a single conversation, pause.
Remember Meera's quiet faith.

Remember the leaders, teachers, healers, and dreamers.
who chose reflection over reaction.
Their ripples reached you;
yours will reach someone else.

Coaching is not a profession — it is a way of being.
To listen deeply.
To hold gently.
To speak truth kindly.
These are the acts that keep the water alive.
They cost nothing — and change everything.

So wherever you go from here —
into a meeting, a classroom, a hospital ward, or a quiet home —
carry this awareness: *you are the next ripple.*
You are the proof that stillness moves.

And when you meet another soul who needs space to breathe,
offer it — without hurry, without fixing, without fear.
Just presence.

That will be enough.

With gratitude for your still water,
Kishore Kumar Thakur

"The ripple does not ask where it will end.
It trusts the pond to remember."

APPENDIX - THE REFLECTION JOURNAL & PROMPTS

A quiet space for your own ripples.

"The pond doesn't ask for words — only attention."

This journal is not meant to be filled quickly.
Treat it as your own pond — return whenever your thoughts grow cloudy, or when a conversation leaves an echo in your heart.
Write slowly. Sometimes one line is enough.

Each chapter corresponds to one ripple of presence — the journey from awareness to stillness — and closes with prompts for reflection, journaling, or dialogue.

🪶 The Stone – Awareness

"Change begins when you notice you are moving."

Awareness is the first ripple — it starts with noticing, not fixing. When you pause long enough to see yourself clearly, the story begins to change.

Reflection Prompts

- What am I bringing into this moment — emotion, intention, or noise?

- Where does my attention live most of the day — past, present, or future?
- What situations make me forget myself?
- When did I last feel completely present with another person?
- What part of me is asking to be seen right now?

Writing Practice:
At the end of each day, write one line beginning with:

"Today I became aware that..."

💧 The Water – Listening

"Listening is how we lend dignity to another's experience."

Listening is the most generous act of leadership.
It transforms silence from emptiness into invitation.

Reflection Prompts

- When was the last time I truly listened without preparing my response?
- What helps me stay curious when I disagree?
- Who in my life needs to be heard more deeply right now?
- What does silence feel like in my body — tense or peaceful?
- What truth have I heard recently that changed how I see?

Writing Practice:
Describe one recent conversation.
Then write:

"What I heard between the words was..."

◈ The Ripple – Trust

"Trust is the quiet confidence that life will find its rhythm."

Trust allows people to unfold at their own pace.
It is the courage to stop managing every outcome.

Reflection Prompts

- What situations tempt me to control others or myself?
- How do I react when I don't know the answer?
- Who has trusted me enough to grow in their own way?
- How can I replace advice with curiosity this week?
- What am I afraid will happen if I truly let go?

Writing Practice:
Complete this sentence each morning:

"Today, I choose to trust that…"

◈ The Current – Integrity

"Integrity is alignment between what we know and what we do."

Integrity is the invisible architecture of peace.
It is how our presence earns quiet respect.

Reflection Prompts

- What values guide my choices when no one is watching?
- When did I last feel "off" — and what truth was I ignoring?
- How do I respond when my principles are tested?
- Where am I being asked to be braver in alignment?
- What does ethical leadership mean to me now?

Writing Practice:

Each Sunday evening, write two short lists:

- *Moments I was in alignment*

Moments I drifted away

Close with one line: *"Next week, I will return to…"*

The Depth – Stillness

"Stillness is not withdrawal; it is wholeness unhurried."

Stillness is the final ripple — not the end of motion, but the mastery of it.

It is where everything you've practiced becomes natural, effortless, human.

Reflection Prompts

- What restores me when I feel scattered?
- When was the last time I experienced peace in action?
- What helps me release the need to be right, seen, or busy?
- How can I bring stillness into my team, my family, or my coaching sessions?
- What does enough feel like to me?

Writing Practice:

End your week by sitting quietly for three minutes.

Then finish the line:

"In stillness, I remembered that…"

◈ Optional Group Practice – The Circle of Reflection

Once a month, gather with peers or colleagues.
Sit in a circle.
Each person shares briefly:

- *One awareness from the month,*
- *One ripple they noticed they created,*
- *One intention they want to carry forward.*

No advice, no fixing. Only listening.
This is how culture remembers.

Closing Page

Write a letter to yourself — the one who first began this book.

What has shifted in your listening, your leading, your being?

Seal it in an envelope, or simply close this page.
The pond will remember. *

ACKNOWLEDGEMENTS

Gratitude is the quiet ripple that never stops returning.

This book began as a whisper — a question, really — about what happens when we stop speaking long enough to listen.
It grew, slowly and gently, through the voices and silences of many people who walked beside me.

To every leader, coach, and learner who trusted me with their stories —
thank you.
Your courage to be seen, your willingness to pause,
and your openness to transformation gave these pages their pulse.

To the mentors and teachers who asked better questions than they answered —
you taught me that guidance is not direction,
but presence.

To my coaching peers and community —
thank you for the conversations that reminded me
that wisdom is shared, not owned.

To my family — for your patience with my long silences,
and for never mistaking reflection for distance.
You've been my first circle,
and the calm beneath every ripple I create.

To the friends who believed in this book
before it even had a name —
thank you for listening when I spoke about ponds, stones, and ripples
as if they were people.

And to the readers —
you, holding this book now —
thank you for slowing down enough to meet me here.
May these words become your own reflection.
May you drop your own stone.

Finally, to the quiet spaces —
the still mornings, the pauses between thoughts,
the water itself —
thank you for teaching me
that silence is not empty.
It is full of beginnings.

If this book has touched you, pass it on.
Every reader becomes the next ripple.

ABOUT THE AUTHOR

Kishore Kumar Thakur is a leadership coach, facilitator, and writer whose work lies at the intersection of reflection, purpose, and human connection.

Drawing on two decades of experience in leadership development and coaching, Kishore helps individuals and organizations cultivate cultures of listening, trust, and conscious presence.

He believes that true change begins not with action, but with awareness — a principle that inspired this fable.

Kishore's approach combines Eastern contemplative wisdom with modern coaching science.

He has worked with leaders across industries to help them slow down, notice deeply, and lead with integrity and compassion.

When not coaching or writing, Kishore can often be found walking by quiet water, sketching ideas in notebooks, or exploring how silence teaches better than words.

The Stone and the Pond is his invitation to every reader — to pause, to listen, and to let their own ripples move through the world with kindness.

Connect: https://www.linkedin.com/in/leadwithkishore/